D0506071

THE
COCKTAIL
GODDESS'S
COMPANION

An Hachette UK Company
www.hachette.co.uk

First published in Great Britain in 2018 by Pyramid,
an imprint of Octopus Publishing Group Ltd
Carmelite House, 50 Victoria Embankment, London EC4Y 0DZ
www.octopusbooks.co.uk

ISBN 978-0-7537-3314-1

A CIP catalogue record for this book is available from the British Library

Printed and bound in China

10 9 8 7 6 5 4 3 2 1

Publisher: Lucy Pessell
Designer: Lisa Layton
Editor: Sarah Vaughan
Production Manager: Caroline Alberti

The measure that has been used in the recipes is based on a bar jigger, which is 25 ml (1 fl oz).
If preferred, a different volume can be used, providing the proportions are kept constant within
a drink and suitable adjustments are made to spoon measurements, where they occur.

Standard level spoon measurements are used in all recipes.
1 tablespoon = one 15 ml spoon
1 teaspoon = one 5 ml spoon

This book contains cocktails made with raw or lightly cooked eggs. It is prudent for more
vulnerable people to avoid uncooked or lightly cooked cocktails made with eggs.

Some of this material previously appeared in The Classic Cocktail Bible.

THE
COCKTAIL
GODDESS'S
COMPANION

MUSINGS & BOOZINGS
A RECIPE BOOK OF CLASSIC COCKTAILS

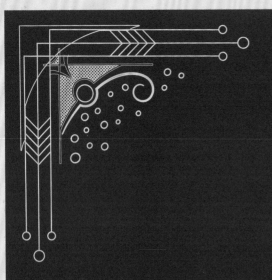

CONTENTS

INTRODUCTION

Who doesn't feel gorgeous and glamorous when they have an expertly mixed Martini in their hand? From the decadent 1920s, when bartenders took the sting out of Prohibition liquor by mixing it with more palatable flavours, to the over indulgence of the 1980s and the cool cocktail chic of the noughties, cocktails have long had a part to play in party people's social lives. With their exotic names, their indulgent ingredients and the care and attention required to create them, it's no surprise that these drinks have remained exclusive and exciting, and are constantly evolving.

ART IN A GLASS

Cocktails should taste every bit as good as they look, which is why bartenders spend years perfecting the art of the perfect blend of ingredients. Tiny tweaks to measurements can make all the difference, and a good cocktail is the result of careful measuring and mixing of very specific ingredients. So don't be tempted to simply empty all those leftover bottles of holiday booze into pretty glasses – cocktail making requires skill and precision, a basic knowledge of spirits and mixers and a lightness of touch.

CLASSICS & NEWCOMERS

The wonderful thing about cocktails is that classic recipes like the Martini, Zombie and Old-fashioned are as popular today as when they were first sipped in the lounge bars of fancy hotels around the world. These drinks have achieved cult status, but they're not too high and mighty to keep the newcomers banished from our bar menus. Mixologists are constantly creating new concoctions and the infinite combination of spirits, mixers, juices, syrups and decorations means that the only limit to the range of cocktails in a bar is the imagination of the bartender. But you don't need to flash your cash in a fancy joint to enjoy the glitz of a cocktail evening: you can create your own drinks at home. With a bit of forward planning, some essential equipment and a few choice recipes up your sleeve, you can become a mixologist for the night, and shake and stir to your heart's content.

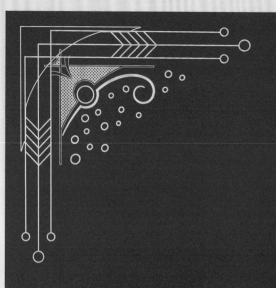

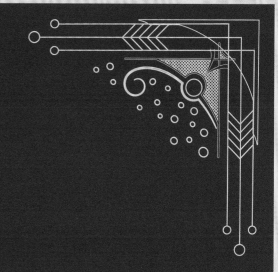

VODKA

SEA BREEZE

ice cubes
2 measures vodka
4 measures cranberry juice
2 measures fresh pink grapefruit juice
2 lime wedges

Put some ice cubes into a highball or hurricane glass. Pour over the vodka and fruit juices. Squeeze the lime wedges into the drink and stir lightly before serving.

SCREWDRIVER

2–3 ice cubes
1½ measures vodka
fresh orange juice, to top up

Put the ice cubes into a highball glass. Pour over the vodka, top up with orange juice and stir lightly, then serve.

The Harvey Wallbanger was named after a Californian surfer in the 1960s, who drank so many of this cocktail that he banged and bounced off the bar walls on his way out.

HARVEY WALLBANGER

6 ice cubes
1 measure vodka
3 measures fresh orange juice
1–2 teaspoons Galliano
orange wheels, to garnish

Put half the ice cubes into a cocktail shaker and the remainder into a highball glass. Add the vodka and orange juice to the shaker and shake until a frost forms on the outside of the shaker. Strain over the ice in the glass. Float the Galliano on top. Garnish with orange wheels and serve with straws.

If the Ancient Persians made decisions whilst drunk, they had a rule to consider it when sober. If they decided on something when sober, they would reconsider it while drunk. Sounds like the kind of logic we should all apply to our decision-making processes.

VODKA SAZERAC

1 white sugar cube
2 drops Angostura bitters
3 drops Pernod
2–3 ice cubes
2 measures vodka
lemonade, to top up

Put the sugar cube into a rocks glass and shake the bitters on to it. Add the Pernod and swirl it around to coat the inside of the glass. Add the ice cubes and pour over the vodka. Top up with lemonade and stir lightly, then serve.

BLOODY MARY

ice cubes
2 measures vodka
I dash fresh lemon juice
Worcestershire sauce, to taste
tomato juice, to top up
½ teaspoon cayenne pepper
salt and pepper
celery stalks, to garnish

Put some ice cubes into a highball glass. Pour over the vodka and lemon juice, add Worcestershire sauce to taste and top up with tomato juice. Add the cayenne pepper and season to taste with salt and pepper. Stir to chill. Garnish with celery stalks and serve.

The legendary "Pete" Petoit, who worked at the famous Harry's New York Bar in Paris after World War I, was the inventor of the Bloody Mary.

BLUE MOON

· · · · · · · · · · · · · · · ·

5–6 ice cubes, cracked
¾ measure vodka
¾ measure tequila
I measure blue Curaçao
lemonade, to top up

Put half the cracked ice into a mixing glass. Add the vodka, tequila and blue Curaçao and stir to mix. Put the remaining ice into a tall glass and strain in the cocktail. Top up with lemonade and serve with a straw.

When Russia banned the sale of vodka during World War I, the government promptly lost a third of its income.

· · · · · · · · · · · · · · · ·

Cenosillicaphobia is a real phobia and means fear of an empty glass.

The Collins takes its name from its creator, John Collins. He first mixed the drink in the early 19th century at Limmer's Hotel in London.

VODKA COLLINS

6 ice cubes
2 measures vodka
juice of 1 lime
1 teaspoon caster sugar
soda water, to top up
lemon or lime wheels and a
maraschino cherry, to garnish

Put half the ice cubes into a cocktail shaker. Add the vodka, lime juice and sugar and shake until a frost forms on the outside of the shaker. Strain into a large highball glass, add the remaining ice cubes and top up with soda water. Garnish with lemon or lime wheels and a maraschino cherry and serve.

COSMOPOLITAN

6 ice cubes, cracked
I measure vodka
½ measure Cointreau
I measure cranberry juice
juice of ½ lime
orange rind twist, to garnish

Put the cracked ice into a cocktail shaker. Add all the remaining ingredients and shake until a frost forms on the outside of the shaker. Strain into a chilled Martini glass. Garnish with an orange rind twist and serve.

"I'd like a cheeseburger, large fries and a Cosmopolitan."

Carrie Bradshaw, *Sex and the City*

GREEN ISLAND QUIET SUNDAY

4–6 ice cubes, plus crushed ice to serve
1 measure vodka
4 measures orange juice
3 dashes Amaretto di Saronno
few drops of grenadine

Put the ice cubes with the vodka, orange juice and Amaretto into a cocktail shaker and shake well. Strain into a highball glass filled with crushed ice, then add a few drops of grenadine.

✳

"With all respect to James Bond, a Martini should be stirred, not shaken."

Kingsley Amis, *Everyday Drinking*

The Moscow Mule was invented in 1941 by an employee of a US drinks firm in conjunction with a Los Angeles bar owner who was overstocked with ginger beer.

MOSCOW MULE

3–4 ice cubes, cracked
2 measures vodka
juice of 2 limes
ginger beer, to top up
lime or orange wheels, to garnish

Put the cracked ice into a cocktail shaker. Add the vodka and lime juice and shake until a frost forms on the outside of the shaker. Pour, without straining, into a highball glass, top up with ginger beer and stir lightly. Garnish with lime or orange wheels and serve.

The Martini glass is the classic cocktail glass and it's used for so much more than just Martinis so it won't sit in the back of the cupboard gathering dust. With its distinctive triangular shape and delicate stem, it's sophisticated enough to play host to the most extravagant drink in your repertoire.

XANTIPPE

4–5 ice cubes
1 measure cherry brandy
1 measure yellow Chartreuse
2 measures vodka

Put the ice cubes into a mixing glass. Pour over the cherry brandy, Chartreuse and vodka and stir vigorously. Strain into a chilled Martini glass, then serve.

Chartreuse is a herb-based liqueur named after a Carthusian monastery near Grenoble in France where it was first made. Yellow Chartreuse has a lower alcohol content than green Chartreuse.

Although "the quick brown fox jumps over the lazy dog" is considered to be the shortest sentence that includes all the letters of the alphabet, alcohol lovers came up with one of their own: "Pack my box with five dozen liquor jugs".

NEW DAY

4–5 ice cubes
3 measures vodka
I measure Calvados
I measure apricot brandy
juice of ½ orange
orange wedge, to garnish

Put the ice cubes into a cocktail shaker. Add all the remaining ingredients and shake until a frost forms on the outside of the shaker. Strain into a rocks glass, garnish with an orange wedge and serve.

GINGERSNAP

2–3 ice cubes
3 measures vodka
I measure ginger wine
soda water, to top up

Put the ice cubes into a rocks glass. Pour over the vodka and ginger wine and stir lightly. Top up with soda water and serve.

The Swahili word "dawa" means something between a medicine and a magic potion. It is traditionally served with a wooden muddler to release more lime juice and adjust the flavour.

DAWA

1 lime, quartered and thickly sliced
1 tablespoon thick honey
1 teaspoon caster sugar
2–3 ice cubes
2 measures vodka

Put the lime slices, honey and sugar into a rocks glass and muddle together Add the ice cubes and pour over the vodka, then serve.

RISING SUN

ice cubes
2 measures vodka
2 teaspoons passion fruit syrup
3 measures grapefruit juice
pink grapefruit slice, to garnish

Put some of the ice cubes with the vodka, passion fruit syrup and grapefruit juice into a shaker and shake to mix. Strain into a rocks glass over 6–8 ice cubes. Garnish with a pink grapefruit slice.

When preparing a muddled drink such as a Mojito or Dawa, gently press down on the ingredients with the muddler and only give the muddler a half-turn. Repeat this a few times. This releases flavour, but doesn't crush the fruit or herbs too much.

BLACK RUSSIAN

4–6 ice cubes, cracked
2 measures vodka
1 measure Kahlúa
chocolate stick, to garnish
(optional)

Put the cracked ice into a rocks glass. Pour over the vodka and Kahlúa and stir. Garnish with a chocolate stick, if you like, and serve.

This is the original cocktail, dating back to the 1950s. Nowadays, it is often served as a long drink, topped up with chilled cola.

This modern take on the Black Russian uses Tia Maria and cream to give the drink its distinctive colour and texture.

WHITE RUSSIAN

6 ice cubes, cracked
1 measure vodka
1 measure Tia Maria
1 measure full-fat milk or double cream

Put half the cracked ice into a cocktail shaker and put the remaining cracked ice into a highball glass. Add all the remaining ingredients to the shaker and shake until a frost forms on the outside of the shaker. Strain over the ice in the glass. Serve with a straw.

27

The hurricane glass is so-called because its shape is similar to the hurricane lamp. It's the perfect glass for tropical punches or long, creamy cocktails.

PARROT'S HEAD PUNCH

ice cubes
1½ measures vodka
1 measure passion fruit liqueur
2 measures watermelon juice
1 measure cranberry juice
1½ measures fresh pink grapefruit juice
pink grapefruit wheel, to garnish

Fill a hurricane glass with ice cubes. Build all the remaining ingredients, one by one in order, over the ice and garnish with a pink grapefruit wheel. Serve with long straws.

BELLINI-TINI

4–5 ice cubes, cracked
2 measures vodka
½ measure peach schnapps
1 teaspoon peach juice
chilled Champagne, to top up
peach slices, to garnish

Put the cracked ice into a cocktail shaker. Add the vodka, schnapps and peach juice and shake until a frost forms on the outside of the shaker. Strain into a chilled Martini glass and top up with chilled Champagne. Garnish with peach slices and serve.

The Bellini was first created in Harry's Bar in Venice about 70 years ago. The bartender named his drink after the Italian artist Giovanni Bellini.

PDQ

4–5 ice cubes

1½ measures chilli-flavoured vodka

1 measure vodka

2 measures chilled beef bouillon

1 tablespoon fresh lemon juice

dash of Tabasco sauce

dash of Worcestershire sauce

salt and black pepper

lemon slice and bottled chilli, to garnish

Put the ice cubes into a cocktail shaker. Pour the vodkas, bouillon and lemon juice over the ice and dash in the Tabasco and Worcestershire sauces. Shake until a frost forms, then strain into a hurricane glass. Season to taste with salt and pepper and garnish with a slice of lemon and a chilli.

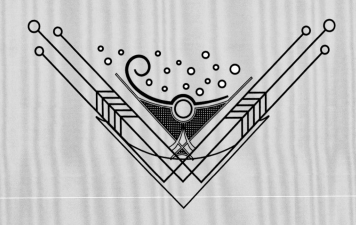

Sweet and with a pronounced flavour of ripe peaches, créme de peche is one of the more unusual fruit liqueurs.

PARSON'S NOSE

2 measures vodka
½ measure Amaretto di Saronno
½ measure crème de peche
1 measure Angostura bitters

Stir the ingredients in a mixing glass, then strain into a chilled Martini glass and serve.

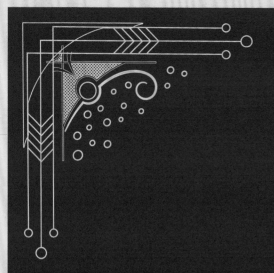

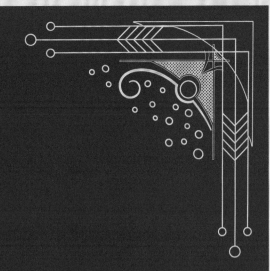

RUM

Said to have been
named for the effect it
had on drinkers, the
Zombie first appeared
in the late 1930s at
Don the Beachcomber,
a popular Polynesian-
themed restaurant in
Hollywood.

ZOMBIE

ice cubes
1 measure dark rum
1 measure white rum
½ measure golden rum
½ measure apricot brandy
juice of ½ lime
1 teaspoon grenadine
2 measures pineapple juice
½ measure sugar syrup
2 teaspoons over-proof rum
pineapple wedge and leaf and
sugar, to garnish

Put some ice cubes with the first 3 rums, apricot brandy, lime juice, grenadine, pineapple juice and sugar syrup into a cocktail shaker and shake well. Pour into a chilled glass without straining and float the overproof rum on top. Garnish with a pineapple wedge and leaf, and sprinkle a pinch of sugar over the top.

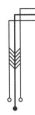

TIKI TREAT

crushed ice
½ ripe mango, peeled and stoned,
plus extra to garnish
3 coconut chunks
I measure coconut cream
2 measures aged rum
dash fresh lemon juice
I teaspoon caster sugar

Put a small scoop of crushed ice with all the other ingredients into a food processor or blender and blend until smooth. Serve in a hurricane glass with long straws and garnish with mango slices.

HAVANA BEACH

½ lime
2 measures pineapple juice
I measure white rum
I teaspoon sugar
dry ginger ale, to top up
lime slice, to garnish

Cut the lime into 4 pieces and put in a food processor or blender with the pineapple juice, rum and sugar. Blend until smooth. Pour into a hurricane glass and top up with dry ginger ale. Garnish with a lime slice.

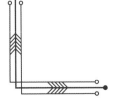

The origin of the word "rum" isn't certain, although one theory is that it comes from "rumbullion", which means "a great tumult or uproar".

SERENADE

. . . .

6 ice cubes, crushed
I measure white rum
½ measure Amaretto di Saronno
½ measure coconut cream
2 measures pineapple juice
pineapple slice, to garnish

Put half the ice into a food processor or blender, add the rum, Amaretto, coconut cream and pineapple juice and blend for 20 seconds. Pour into a tall glass over the remaining ice cubes. Garnish with a pineapple slice and serve with a straw.

The Mai Tai, which takes its name from the Tahitian word "maita'i", meaning "good", is thought to have been invented at Trader Vic's restaurant in Oakland, California, in 1944.

MAI TAI

ice cubes
crushed ice
2 measures golden rum
½ measure orange Curaçao
½ measure orgeat syrup
juice of 1 lime
2 teaspoons Wood's Navy Rum
lime rind spiral and mint sprig,
to garnish

Half–fill a cocktail shaker with ice cubes and put some crushed ice into a rocks glass. Add the golden rum, Curaçao, orgeat syrup and lime juice to the shaker and shake until a frost forms on the outside of the shaker. Strain over the ice in the glass. Float the Navy Rum on top Garnish with a lime rind spiral and a mint sprig and serve.

BAHAMAS PUNCH

juice of 1 lemon
1 teaspoon sugar syrup
3 drops Angostura bitters
½ teaspoon grenadine
3 measures golden or white rum
orange and lemon slices
ice cubes, cracked
grated nutmeg, to garnish

Pour the lemon juice and sugar syrup into a mixing glass. Shake in the bitters, then add the grenadine, rum and fruit. Stir and chill. To serve, fill a rocks glass with cracked ice, pour in the punch without straining and sprinkle with grated nutmeg.

Over-proof rum is a high-strength, potent rum which is mostly used in layered cocktails as a floating top layer.

THE
PAPA DOBLE

crushed ice

3 measures white rum

½ measure maraschino liqueur

1 measure fresh lime juice

1 ½ measures fresh grapefruit juice

grapefruit wedge, to garnish

Put the crushed ice into a blender. Add all the remaining ingredients and blend on high speed until smooth. Pour into a highball glass. Garnish with a grapefruit wedge and serve with straws.

The Papa Doble was Ernest Hemingway's famed tipple. It can be sweetened with half a measure of sugar syrup and downscaled to two measures of rum, if desired.

Hemingway had a small bar built
in his fishing boat and lovingly
referred to tequila as
"the steering liquor."

TELFORD

4–5 ice cubes
1 measure white rum
1 measure dark rum
½ measure tequila
½ measure Cointreau
1 measure apricot brandy
1 measure fresh
orange juice
2–3 drops orange bitters
1 dash grenadine
cocktail cherries, to garnish

Put the ice cubes into a cocktail shaker. Pour the rums, tequila, Cointreau, apricot brandy, orange juice, bitters and grenadine over the ice and shake until a frost forms. Strain into a Martini glass and garnish with cherries.

41

Eighteenth-century sailors were often paid in rum. To test the rum's authenticity, they allegedly mixed it with gunpowder – successful ignition indicated authenticity.

HUMMINGBIRD

4–5 ice cubes, crushed
I measure dark rum
I measure light rum
I measure Southern Comfort
I measure fresh orange juice
cola, to top up
orange slice, to garnish

Put the crushed ice into a cocktail shaker. Pour the rums, Southern Comfort and orange juice over the ice and shake until a frost forms. Strain into a long glass and top up with cola. Garnish with an orange slice and serve with a straw.

SPICED SIDECAR

ice cubes
juice of ½ lemon
1 measure Morgan Spiced Rum
1 measure brandy
1 measure Cointreau
lemon and orange rind twists,
to garnish

Half-fill a cocktail shaker with ice cubes and fill a rocks glass with ice cubes. Add all the remaining ingredients to the shaker and shake until a frost forms on the outside of the shaker. Strain over the ice in the glass. Garnish with lemon and orange rind.

PIÑA COLADA

1 scoop crushed ice
2 measures white rum
2 teaspoons fresh lime juice
2 measures coconut cream
2 measures pineapple juice
1 scoop vanilla ice cream
pineapple leaf, to garnish

Put the crushed ice into a blender. Add all the remaining ingredients and blend on high speed for 20–30 seconds. Pour into a highball glass, garnish with a pineapple leaf and serve.

This world-famous cocktail was created by a bartender in Puerto Rico in 1957. It is a homage to the exotic flavours of the country.

ST LUCIA

4–5 ice cubes
1 measure Curaçao
1 measure dry vermouth
juice of ½ orange
1 teaspoon grenadine
2 measures white or golden rum
orange rind spiral and cocktail cherry,
to garnish

Put the ice cubes into a cocktail shaker and pour over the Curaçao, vermouth, orange juice, grenadine and rum. Shake until a frost forms, then pour without straining into a highball glass. Garnish with an orange rind spiral and a cherry.

BLUE HAWAIIAN

1 scoop crushed ice
1 measure white rum
½ measure blue Curaçao
2 measures pineapple juice
1 measure coconut cream
pineapple wedge, to garnish

Put the crushed ice into a blender. Add all the remaining ingredients and blend on high speed for 20–30 seconds. Pour into a chilled Martini glass. Garnish with a pineapple wedge and serve.

Rum has been known by various other names, including "Barbados Water", "Red Eye", "Devil's Death" and "Nelson's Blood". The last because it was believed that Admiral Nelson's body was carried back to England in a barrel of rum.

DAIQUIRI

ice cubes, cracked
juice of 2 limes
1 teaspoon sugar syrup
3 measures white rum
lime wheel, to garnish

Put plenty of cracked ice into a cocktail shaker. Add all the remaining ingredients and shake until a frost forms on the outside of the shaker. Strain into a chilled Martini glass. Garnish with a lime wheel and serve.

The much loved Daiquiri is refreshing combination of white rum, lime and sugar, invented in the early 20th century by Jennings S. Cox, an American working in the mines of the Cuban town of Daiquirí.

MOJITO

12 mint leaves, plus an extra sprig to garnish

½ measure sugar syrup

4 lime wedges

crushed ice

2 measures white rum

soda water, to top up

Put the mint, sugar syrup and lime wedges into a highball glass and muddle together. Fill the glass with crushed ice, pour over the rum and stir. Top up with soda water. Garnish with a mint sprig and serve with straws.

Apparently another favourite of Ernest Hemingway. He made the bar called La Bodeguita del Medio famous by writing "My mojito in La Bodeguita, My daiquiri in El Floridita" on a wall in the bar.
Or so the legend goes. Not everyone is convinced.

Planter's Punch was created by Fred L. Myers in the late 19th century. For a modern fruity version, substitute pineapple juice for the water.

PLANTER'S PUNCH

ice cubes

2 measures Myer's Jamaican Planter's Punch Rum

4 drops Angostura bitters

½ measure fresh lime juice

2 measures iced water

1 measure sugar syrup

orange and lime wheels, to garnish

Half-fill a cocktail shaker with ice cubes and fill a highball glass with ice cubes. Add all the remaining ingredients to the shaker and shake until a frost forms on the outside of the shaker. Strain over the ice in the glass. Garnish with orange and lime wheels and serve.

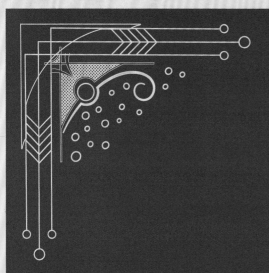

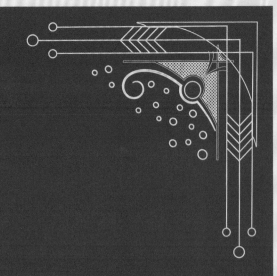

GIN

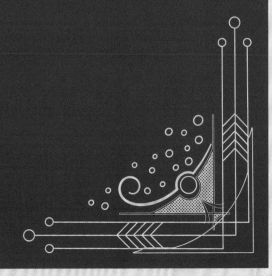

The now legendary Singapore Sling was created by Ngiam Tong Boon, a bartender at the Long Bar in Raffles Hotel, Singapore, around 1915.

SINGAPORE SLING

ice cubes
1 measure gin
½ measure cherry brandy
¼ measure Cointreau
¼ measure Bénédictine
½ measure grenadine
½ measure fresh lime juice
5 measures pineapple juice
1 dash Angostura bitters
pineapple slice and cocktail cherry, to garnish

Put some ice cubes with all the other ingredients into a cocktail shaker and shake well. Strain over ice cubes in a tall glass. Garnish with a pineapple slice and a cherry.

GIN SLING

4–5 ice cubes
juice of ½ lemon
1 measure cherry brandy
3 measures gin
soda water, to top up
maraschino cherry and a lemon slice, to garnish

Put the ice cubes into a cocktail shaker. Add the lemon juice, cherry brandy and gin and shake until a frost forms on the outside of the shaker. Pour, without straining, into a highball glass and top up with soda water. Garnish with a maraschino cherry and a lemon slice and serve with straws.

This popular relative of the classic Singapore Sling is a deliciously refreshing long drink with a piquant flavour courtesy of the lemon juice.

CLASSIC DRY MARTINI

. . . .

½ measure dry vermouth

3 measures ice-cold gin

green olive or lemon rind twist, to garnish

Swirl the vermouth around the inside of a chilled Martini glass, then discard the excess. Pour in the ice-cold gin and add an olive or lemon rind twist.

"I like to have a Martini,
Two at the very most.
After three I'm under the table,
after four I'm under my host."

. . . .

Dorothy Parker

This most famous cocktail
of all was invented at the
Knickerbocker Hotel in
New York, 1910.

CLOVER CLUB

4–5 ice cubes
juice of 1 lime
½ teaspoon sugar syrup
1 egg white
3 measures gin
lime rind, to garnish

Put the ice cubes into a cocktail shaker. Add all the remaining ingredients and shake until a frost forms on the outside of the shaker. Strain the cocktail into a highball glass. Garnish with lime rind and serve.

This cocktail came into being at the bar of Bellevue-Stratford Hotel in Philadelphia, the meeting place of a group of men called The Clover Club, from which the cocktail takes its name.

PINK CLOVER CLUB

4–5 ice cubes
juice of 1 lime
1 dash grenadine
1 egg white
3 measures gin
strawberry slice, to garnish

Put the ice cubes into a cocktail shaker. Pour the lime juice, grenadine, egg white and gin over the ice. Shake until a frost forms, then strain into a Martini glass. Garnish with a strawberry slice and serve with a straw.

PINK GIN

1–4 dashes Angostura bitters
1 measure gin
iced water, to top up

Shake the bitters into a Martini glass and swirl around to coat the inside of the glass. Add the gin and top up with iced water to taste, then serve.

NEGRONI

ice cubes
1 measure Plymouth Gin
1 measure Campari
1 measure red vermouth
soda water, to top up (optional)
orange slice, to garnish

Put some ice cubes into a mixing glass and fill a rocks glass with ice cubes. Add the gin, Campari and vermouth to the mixing glass, stir briefly to mix and strain over the ice in the glass. Top up with soda water, if you like. Garnish with an orange slice and serve.

An American GI called Negroni stationed in Italy during World War II wanted an extra kick to his Americano cocktail, so the bartender added gin and this cocktail was born.

Created in the mid-19th century, fizzes are long, gently sparkling drinks, traditionally made with a spirit, lemon juice and sugar, and topped up with a fizzy drink.

GIN FIZZ

ice cubes
2 measures Plymouth Gin
I measure fresh lemon juice
2–3 dashes sugar syrup
¼ egg white, beaten
soda water, to top up
lemon wheels and mint sprig, to garnish

Half-fill a cocktail shaker with ice cubes. Add the gin, lemon juice, sugar syrup and egg white and shake briefly to mix. Strain into a highball glass and top up with soda water. Garnish with lemon wheels and a mint sprig and serve.

The Martini purist mixes their tipple with an almost religious fervour. So if you prefer a cocktail onion in your drink rather than an olive, it's a Gibson, not a Martini.

GIBSON

5–6 ice cubes
½ measure dry vermouth
3 measures gin
cocktail onion, to garnish

Put the ice cubes into a mixing glass. Pour over the vermouth and gin and stir vigorously (never shake) and evenly without splashing. Strain into a chilled Martini glass. Garnish with a cocktail onion and serve.

"A perfect Martini should be made by filling a glass with gin then waving it in the general direction of Italy."

Noël Coward

Maraschino cherries are preserved in alcohol and then soaked in sugar and food colourings to give them their distinctive flavour. They're an essential store cupboard item for budding mixologists.

AVIATION

ice cubes
2 measures gin
½ measure maraschino liqueur
½ measure fresh lemon juice
maraschino cherry, to garnish

Half-fill a cocktail shaker with ice cubes. Add all the remaining ingredients and shake until a frost forms on the outside of the shaker. Fine or double strain into a chilled Martini glass. Garnish with a maraschino cherry and serve.

VESPER

. . . .

ice cubes
3 measures gin
I measure vodka
½ measure Lillet Blanc
lemon rind twist, to garnish

Half-fill a cocktail shaker with ice cubes. Add the gin, vodka and Lillet and shake until a frost forms on the outside of the shaker. Strain into a chilled Martini glass. Garnish with a lemon rind twist and serve.

GIMLET

. . . .

2 measures gin
I measure lime cordial
ice cubes
½ measure water
lime wedge, to garnish

Put the gin and lime cordial into a mixing glass, fill up with ice cubes and stir well. Strain into a chilled Martini glass, add the water, then squeeze the lime wedge into the cocktail before adding it to the drink.

TOM COLLINS

2 measures gin
1 ½ teaspoons fresh lemon juice
1 teaspoon sugar syrup
ice cubes
soda water, to top up
lemon wheel, to garnish

Put the gin, lemon juice and sugar syrup into a highball glass, stir well and fill up with ice cubes. Top up with soda water. Garnish with a lemon wheel and serve.

WHITE LADY

1 measure gin
1 measure Cointreau
1 measure fresh lemon juice
lemon rind twist, to garnish

Pour the gin, Cointreau and lemon juice into a cocktail shaker. Shake well, strain into a chilled Martini glass and garnish with a lemon rind twist.

FRENCH '75

ice cubes, cracked
1 measure gin
juice of ½ lemon
1 teaspoon caster sugar
chilled Champagne or sparkling
dry white wine, to top up
orange wheel, to garnish

Half-fill a highball glass with cracked ice. Add the gin, lemon juice and sugar and stir well. Top up with chilled Champagne or sparkling dry white wine. Garnish with an orange wheel and serve.

Created in 1915 at Harry's New York Bar in Paris, the French '75 was said to have a kick like being shelled by a French 75mm field gun.

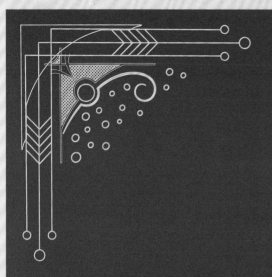

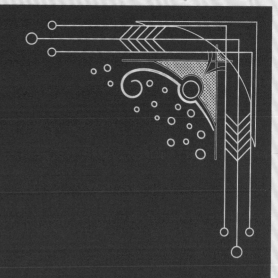

WHISKY

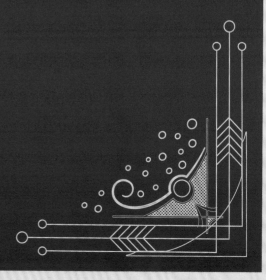

NEW YORKER

2–3 ice cubes, cracked
1 measure Scotch whisky
1 teaspoon fresh lime juice
1 teaspoon icing sugar
finely grated rind of ½ lemon
lemon rind spiral, to garnish

Put the cracked ice into a cocktail shaker and add the whisky, lime juice and sugar. Shake until a frost forms. Strain into a Martini glass. Sprinkle the grated lemon rind over the surface and garnish the rim with a lemon rind spiral.

"Whisky" or "whiskey" is a common spelling conundrum but the correct name is simply determined by where it was made. As a general rule, "whisky" is made in Scotland, Canada and the rest of the world, while Ireland and America use "whiskey". And where whisk(e)y comes from is of great importance to a lot of people in a lot of places.

The Manhattan was reputedly created at New York's Manhattan Club at the request of Sir Winston Churchill's mother, Lady Randolph Churchill, who was hosting a party for a politician.

MANHATTAN

ice cubes
2 measures rye or bourbon whiskey
1 measure extra dry vermouth
4 dashes Angostura bitters
maraschino cherry, to garnish

Put some ice cubes into a mixing glass. Add all the remaining ingredients and stir. Strain into a chilled Martini glass. Garnish with a maraschino cherry and serve.

BOURBON PEACH SMASH

6 mint leaves
3 peach slices
3 lemon slices
2 teaspoons caster sugar
ice cubes
crushed ice
2 measures bourbon whiskey
lemon wedge, to garnish

Put the mint leaves, peach and lemon slices and sugar into a cocktail shaker and muddle together. Half-fill the shaker with ice cubes and put some crushed ice into a rocks glass. Add the bourbon to the shaker and shake until a frost forms on the outside of the shaker. Strain over the ice in the glass. Garnish with a lemon wedge and serve.

Bourbon whiskey is an American whiskey which gets its name from an area of Bourbon County in Kentucky.

MISSISSIPPI PUNCH

. . . .

crushed ice
3 drops Angostura bitters
1 teaspoon sugar syrup
juice of 1 lemon
1 measure brandy
1 measure dark rum
2 measures bourbon whiskey

Half-fill a tall glass with crushed ice. Shake the bitters over the ice. Pour in the sugar syrup and the lemon juice, then stir gently to mix thoroughly. Add the brandy, rum and bourbon, in that order, stir once and serve with straws.

AMERICAN BELLE

. . . .

½ measure cherry liqueur
½ measure Amaretto di Saronno
½ measure bourbon whiskey

Pour the cherry liqueur into a shot glass. Using the back of a bar spoon, slowly float the Amaretto over the cherry liqueur. Pour the bourbon over the Amaretto in the same way.

MINT JULEP

10 mint leaves, plus an extra sprig to garnish
1 teaspoon sugar syrup
4 dashes Angostura bitters
crushed ice
2 measures bourbon whiskey

Put the mint leaves, sugar syrup and bitters into a highball glass and muddle together. Fill the glass with crushed ice. Pour over the bourbon and stir well. Garnish with a mint sprig and serve.

The Mint Julep is the ultimate cocktail of America's Deep South. The earliest written reference dates this aperitif back to 1803.

First produced in the town of Angostura in Venezuela as a cure for seasickness, Angostura bitters is a key ingredient in many cocktails.

VIRGINIA MINT JULEP

9 young mint sprigs, plus extra to garnish
1 teaspoon sugar syrup
crushed ice
3 measures bourbon whiskey

Muddle the mint and sugar syrup in a highball glass. Fill the glass with crushed ice, pour the bourbon over the ice and stir gently. Pack in more crushed ice and stir until a frost forms. Wrap the glass in a table napkin and serve garnished with a mint sprig.

Short for Old-fashioned Whiskey Cocktail, and with the old-fashioned, or rocks, glass named after it, the Old Fashioned is one of those classic cocktails whose authentic recipe is hotly debated.

OLD FASHIONED

2 measures bourbon whiskey
ice cubes
1 teaspoon sugar syrup 4 dashes
Angostura bitters
orange rind twist, to garnish

Pour the bourbon into a rocks glass and add a few ice cubes. Build the sugar syrup and then the bitters over the ice. Garnish with an orange rind twist and serve.

GODFATHER

ice cubes
2 measures J&B Rare Scotch whisky
1 measure Amaretto di Saronno

Put some ice cubes with the whisky and Amaretto into a cocktail shaker and shake vigorously. Strain into a small old-fashioned glass filled with ice cubes.

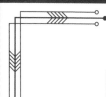

RATTLESNAKE

4–5 ice cubes, plus extra to serve
1½ measures whisky
1 teaspoon fresh lemon juice
1 teaspoon sugar syrup
1 egg white
few drops Pernod

Put all the ingredients into a cocktail shaker and shake extremely well. Strain into a glass and add more ice.

The Rattlesnake first appeared in the 1930 edition of *The Savoy Cocktail Book*, the bartending manual of the Savoy Hotel in London.

WHISKY MAC

3–4 ice cubes
1 measure Scotch whisky
1 measure ginger wine

Put the ice cubes into a rocks glass. Pour over the whisky and ginger wine, stir lightly and serve.

WHISKY SOUR

ice cubes
2 measures whisky
1½ measures fresh lemon juice
1 egg white
2 tablespoons caster sugar
4 dashes Angostura bitters
lemon slice and cocktail cherry, to garnish

Put some ice cubes with the whisky, lemon juice, egg white, sugar and bitters into a shaker and shake well. Strain into a sour glass filled with ice cubes and garnish with a lemon slice and a cherry on a cocktail stick.

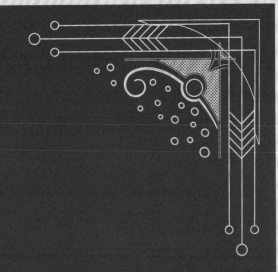

TEQUILA

The Tequila Sunrise, a classic from the 1970s, gets its name from the gradations in colour created as the grenadine sinks down the glass, which mimic the appearance of the sun rising.

TEQUILA SUNRISE

ice cubes
2 measures tequila
4 measures fresh orange juice
2 teaspoons grenadine
orange slices, to garnish

Put some ice cubes with the tequila and orange juice into a cocktail shaker and shake to mix. Strain into a highball glass filled with ice cubes. Slowly pour in the grenadine and allow it to settle. Garnish with an orange slice.

TIJUANA SLING

ice cubes
1¼ measures tequila
¾ measure crème de cassis
¾ measure fresh lime juice
2 dashes Peychaud's bitters
3½ measures dry ginger ale
lime slice and blackcurrants or
blueberries, to garnish

Put some ice cubes and all the ingredients, except the ginger ale, into a cocktail shaker and shake vigorously. Pour into a tall glass, then top up with dry ginger ale. Garnish with a lime slice and some berries.

Created in about 1830 in New Orleans, the Tijuana Sling calls for Peychaud's bitters ... similar to Angostura bitters but with a lighter, sweeter taste.

MARGARITA

1 lime wedge
rock salt
ice cubes
2 measures Herrudura
Reposado Tequila
1 measure fresh lime juice
1 measure triple sec
lime wheel, to garnish

Moisten the rim of a Margarita glass with the lime wedge and frost with the salt. Half-fill a cocktail shaker with ice cubes. Add all the remaining ingredients and shake until a frost forms on the outside of the shaker. Strain into the glass. Garnish with a lime wheel and serve.

FROSTING: Put some lemon or lime juice or water into a saucer and dip the rim of the glass into it. Now dip the glass into the sugar or salt (again, using a saucer), twisting it around for even coverage. Clean excess frosting from the inside of the glass using a lime or lemon wedge. Carefully pour the drink into the centre of the glass so that the frosting remains intact.

There are thirteen minerals that
are essential for human life, and
all of them can be found in alcohol.

GRAND MARGARITA

I lime wedge, plus an extra to garnish

rock salt

ice cubes

1½ measures silver tequila

I measure Grand Marnier

I measure fresh lime juice

Moisten the rim of a
Margarita glass with the
lime wedge and
frost with the salt. Half-
fill a cocktail shaker with
ice cubes. Add all the
remaining ingredients and
shake until a frost forms on
the outside of the shaker.
Fine or double strain into
the glass and garnish with
an extra lime wedge.

83

DESERT DAISY

crushed ice
1 measure tequila
1 ¼ measures fresh lime juice
2 teaspoons sugar syrup
1 tablespoon Fraise de Bois
blackberry, strawberry, lime and
orange wedges and mint sprig, to
garnish

Half-fill a large rocks glass with crushed ice. Pour in the tequila, lime juice and sugar syrup and stir gently until a frost forms. Add more crushed ice then float the Fraise de Bois on top. Garnish with a blackberry, a strawberry, a lime wedge, an orange wedge and a mint sprig.

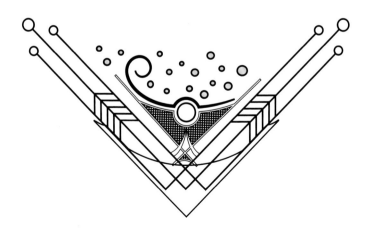

AGAVE JULEP

8 torn mint leaves
1 tablespoon sugar syrup
1 ¼ measures tequila gold
1 ¼ measures fresh lime juice
crushed ice
lime wedge and mint sprig, to garnish

Muddle the mint leaves with the sugar syrup in a highball glass. Add the tequila and lime juice, fill the glass with crushed ice and stir vigorously to mix. Garnish with a lime wedge and a mint sprig.

Contrary to popular belief, the blue agave plant from which tequila is made is a member of the lily family, not the cactus family.

BLOODY MARIA

pepper
celery salt
1 lime wedge
ice cubes
1¼ measures tequila
2 teaspoons medium sherry
2 dashes Tabasco sauce
4 dashes Worcestershire sauce
1 tablespoon fresh lime juice
4 measures tomato juice
cayenne pepper
celery stick, lime wedge and
basil sprig, to garnish

Mix some pepper and celery salt together on a small saucer. Moisten the rim of a rocks glass with the lime wedge, then frost with the pepper and salt mixture. Half-fill a cocktail shaker with ice cubes. Add the tequila, sherry, Tabasco sauce, Worcestershire sauce, lime juice, tomato juice and a pinch each of celery salt, pepper and cayenne pepper. Shake until a frost forms on the outside of the shaker and pour into the glass. Garnish with a celery stick, lime wedge and basil sprig and serve.

> "I'm an occasional drinker, the kind of guy who goes out for a beer and wakes up in Singapore with a full beard."

Raymond Chandler,
Philip Marlowe's Guide To Life

BORDER CROSSING

ice cubes
1½ measures gold tequila
1 measure fresh lime juice
1 measure clear honey
4 dashes orange bitters
3 measures dry ginger ale
blueberries and lime wedges, to garnish

Put some ice cubes with the tequila, lime juice, honey and orange bitters in a cocktail shaker and shake well. Pour into a highball glass and top up with the dry ginger ale. Garnish with blueberries and lime wedges.

BORDER CROSSING

1 lime
1 dash sugar syrup
crushed ice
1 measure José Cuervo Gold tequila
1 measure Kahlúa
dry ginger ale, to top up

Cut the lime into slices, put them into a highball glass and muddle with the sugar syrup. Half-fill the glass with crushed ice and add the tequila and Kahlúa. Stir well, then top up with dry ginger ale.

BRAVE BULL

1 lime
1 dash sugar syrup
crushed ice
1 measure José Cuervo Gold tequila
1 measure Kahlúa
dry ginger ale, to top up

Fill a rocks glass with ice cubes. Pour in the tequila and Kahlúa and stir gently.

BATANGA

1 lime
rock salt
ice cubes
2 measures El Tequileno
Blanco tequila
cola, to top up

Cut the tip off the lime and make a slit in its side. Dip in the salt and run it around the edge of a rocks glass. Fill the glass with ice cubes and add the tequila. Squeeze out half the lime juice, then with the knife used to cut the lime, stir the drink while topping up with cola.

This much-loved cocktail was invented by Don Javier Delgado Corona in his bar in Tequila, Mexico in 1961. Batanga was the nickname of one of his friends.

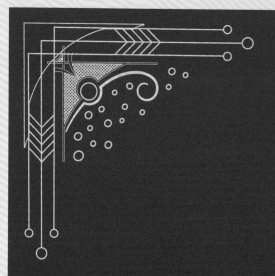

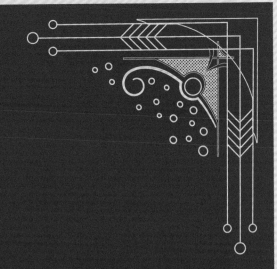

BRANDY

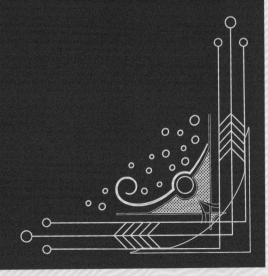

BRANDY SIDECAR

ice cubes
1 measure Cointreau
2 measures brandy
1 measure fresh lemon juice
maraschino cherry and orange
rind spiral, to garnish

Half-fill a cocktail shaker with ice cubes. Add all the remaining ingredients and shake until a frost forms on the outside of the shaker. Strain into a chilled Martini glass. Garnish with a maraschino cherry on a cocktail stick and an orange rind spiral and serve.

The Sidecar was reputedly created at the Ritz Hotel in Paris during World War I for one of the bar's regulars, an army captain who travelled in a motorbike sidecar.

Calvados is an apple brandy from the French region of Lower Normandy. It is made from specially grown apples, both sweet and tart varieties.

PARISIEN

crushed ice
1 measure brandy
½ measure Calvados
1 measure fresh lemon juice
sugar syrup, to taste
½ measure Poire William
apple and pear slices, to garnish

Fill a glass with crushed ice. Add the brandy, Calvados, lemon juice and sugar syrup to taste. Pour the Poire William over the top and garnish with apple and pear slices.

Campari is dark red aperitif which has as its essential ingredient chinotto oranges. Also known as myrtle-leaved oranges, these are small, bitter oranges grown in specific regions of Italy.

LEO

. . . .

2–3 ice cubes, crushed
1 measure brandy
1½ measures fresh orange juice
½ measure Amaretto di Saronno
soda water, to taste
1 teaspoon Campari

Put the crushed ice into a cocktail shaker. Add the brandy, orange juice and Amaretto and shake well. Strain into a tall glass and add soda water to taste and the Campari.

BRANDY ALEXANDER

3 ice cubes, cracked
1 measure brandy
1 measure dark crème de cacao
1 measure single cream
chocolate flake, to garnish

Put the cracked ice into a cocktail shaker. Add all the remaining ingredients and shake until a frost forms on the outside of the shaker. Strain into a chilled Martini glass. Garnish with a sprinkling of chocolate flake and serve.

BRANDY FIX

crushed ice
2 teaspoons sugar syrup
1¼ measures fresh lemon juice
½ measure cherry brandy
1 measure brandy
lemon rind spiral, to garnish

Fill a rocks glass with crushed ice. Build all the ingredients, one by one in order, over the ice. Garnish the cocktail with a lemon rind spiral and serve.

BRANDY CRUSTA

1 lemon wedge
caster sugar
ice cubes
2 measures brandy
½ measure orange Curaçao
½ measure maraschino liqueur
1 measure fresh lemon juice
3 dashes Angostura bitters
lemon rind spiral, to garnish

Moisten the rim of a chilled Martini glass with the lemon wedge and frost with the sugar. Half-fill a cocktail shaker with ice cubes. Add all the remaining ingredients and shake until a frost forms on the outside of the shaker. Strain into the glass. Garnish with a lemon rind spiral and serve.

A Crusta combines a spirit with lemon juice and Angostura bitters and is traditionally served with a lemon rind spiral.

True Curaçao liqueur is made from the dried peels of the "Laraha", a bitter orange native to Curaçao.

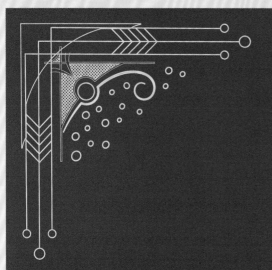

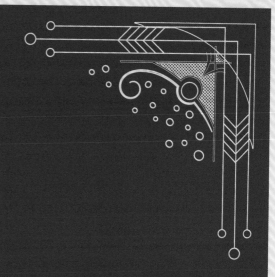

CHAMPAGNE
&
PROSECCO

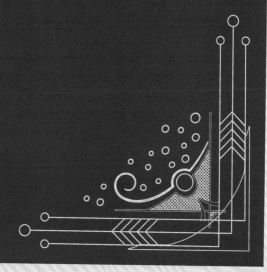

CHAMPAGNE COCKTAIL

1 white sugar cube
1–2 dashes Angostura bitters
1 measure brandy
4 measures chilled Champagne
orange wheel, to garnish

Put the sugar cube into a chilled Martini glass or Champagne flute and saturate with the bitters. Add the brandy, then top up with the chilled Champagne. Garnish with an orange wheel and serve.

GRAND MIMOSA

1 measure Grand Marnier
2 measures fresh orange juice
Champagne, to top up

Pour the Grand Marnier and orange juice into a Champagne flute and top up with chilled Champagne.

BELLINI

2 measures peach juice
4 measures chilled champagne
1 dash grenadine (optional)
peach slice, to garnish (optional)

Mix the peach juice and chilled Champagne in a large Champagne glass with a dash of grenadine, if using. Garnish with a peach slice, if you like.

"I only drink Champagne on two occasions. When I am in love, and when I am not."

Coco Chanel

101

ORCHARD BELLINI

½ ripe white peach
1 measure apple juice
dash of sugar syrup
prosecco, to top up

Add the peach and sugar syrup to a blender or food processor and blend until smooth. Pour into a Champagne flute with the apple juice and the sugar syrup and top with chilled Prosecco.

MANDARIN 75

1 measure Cointreau
½ measure lemon juice
2 teaspoons sugar syrup
prosecco, to top up
orange twist, to garnish

Add the Cointreau, lemon juice and sugar syrup to a chilled Champagne flute. Top with chilled Prosecco and garnish with an orange twist.

> "Too much of anything is bad, but too much Champagne is just right."

F. Scott Fitzgerald

MONTE CARLO SLING

I measure cognac
I measure peach liqueur
I measure orange juice
prosecco, to top up
orange slice, to garnish

Pour the cognac, peach liqueur and orange juice into a highball glass filled with cubed ice. Top with chilled Prosecco and garnish with a slice of orange.

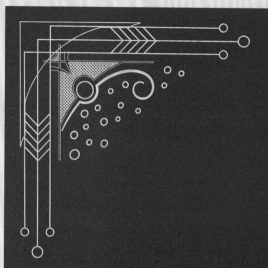

OTHER SPIRITS & LIQUEURS

CAIPIRINHA

1 lime, quartered
2 teaspoons caster sugar
crushed ice
2 measures cachaça

Put the lime quarters and sugar into a rocks glass and muddle together. Fill the glass with crushed ice and pour over the cachaça. Stir and add more ice as desired.

Cachaça, made from sugarcane juice, is the magic ingredient in this Brazillian classic.

Batidas are popular Brazilian cocktails blended from fresh fruit juice and cachaça. The most common variations in Brazil include passion fruit, coconut milk and cashew fruit.

BATIDA

crushed ice
2 measures cachaça
½ measure sugar syrup
½ measure fresh lemon juice
3 measures fresh fruit juice, such as strawberry, pineapple or mango

Fill a highball glass with crushed ice. Pour the cachaça, sugar syrup, lemon juice and fruit juice into the glass and stir to mix thoroughly.

SANGRIA

Serves 10–12

ice cubes
2 bottles light Spanish red wine,
chilled
4 measures brandy (optional)
450ml (¾ pint) soda water, chilled
fruit in season, such as apples, pears,
lemons, peaches and strawberries,
sliced orange slices, to garnish

Put some ice cubes into a large bowl and pour over the wine and brandy, if using. Stir. Add the soda water and float the fruit on top. Serve in tall glasses and garnish with orange slices.

PIMM'S COCKTAIL

ice cubes
1 measure Pimm's No. 1 Cup
1 measure gin
2 measures lemonade
2 measures ginger ale
cucumber strips, blueberries and
orange wheels, to garnish

Fill a highball glass with ice cubes. Build all the remaining ingredients, one by one in order, over the ice. Garnish with cucumber strips, blueberries and orange wheels and serve.

LONG ISLAND ICED TEA

ice cubes
½ measure vodka
½ measure gin
½ measure white rum
½ measure tequila
½ measure Cointreau
½ measure fresh lemon juice
cola, to top up
lemon wedge, to garnish

Half-fill a cocktail shaker with ice cubes and fill a highball glass with ice cubes. Add the vodka, gin, rum, tequila, Cointreau and lemon juice to the shaker and briefly shake to mix. Strain over the ice in the glass. Top up with cola. Garnish with a lemon wedge.

A very potent brew, supposedly created by Robert "Rosebud" Butt of the Oak Beach Inn, Hampton Bay.

INDEX